Dwayne 'The Rock' Johnson

The Life, Lessons & Rules for Success

Influential Individuals

Table of Contents

Introduction

What kind of individual moves on from a failed professional football career into one of the greatest professional wrestlers of all time, and then onto becoming Hollywood's most bankable movie star?

The best way to answer that question is to look at the life of a man who has done all that; Dwayne "The Rock" Johnson. To the world, Dwayne Johnson is a million-dollar star with the physique of a demigod and a tough talking demeanor. Many also know him as a former wrestling superstar. He has dominated every sector of pop culture that he has elbowed his way into – wrestling, television, movies, comedy, even coveting the sexiest man alive. However, Dwayne Johnson was not born into greatness.

In this book, we take an in-depth look into the life of Dwayne Johnson. We explore the childhood of Dwayne Johnson, his brushes with the law as a teenager, the kind of problems his family went through during his teenage years, his failed football career, his bouts with depression, his foray into the wrestling industry, and how he managed to turn his wrestling popularity into a million dollar acting career, as well as his personal life. Finally, we take a look at the defining moments in Dwayne Johnson's life and how they helped him become the man he is today. Not only will this book give you clear insights into the life of Dwayne Johnson, it will also help you understand the drive, determination and grit that helped conquer every field he's been involved in.

Are you ready to take a journey through life in the shoes of Dwayne "The Rock" Johnson? Let's get started.

Chapter One: Early Life

"Don't be afraid to be ambitious about your goals. Hard work never stops. Neither should your dreams." – Dwayne Johnson

American pro wrestler, actor and producer Dwayne "The Rock" Johnson is one of the world's biggest pop culture icons. His signature smile and ripped physique are well-known all over the world. He's one of the world's top paid actors, alongside other famous action stars like Tom Cruise and Jackie Chan. He is one of WWE's greatest superstars, having won the World Wrestling Championships a record 10 times. He has starred in popular films like *The Scorpion King* and *The Fast and the Furious* franchise. He even won the 2016 title of the sexiest man alive.

To the world, The Rock is a star whose charm and charisma have captured the hearts of audiences all over the world, from his days as a pro wrestler to his foray into acting. However, what many do not know is that The Rock has not always had everything going for him. Behind the massive success that the actor has achieved is a tale of hard work, grit, and a strong determination to achieve success, no matter what it takes. From arrests, injury and bouts of depression, there were several instances that threatened to stop The Rock from becoming the man that he is today.

Dwayne Douglas Johnson came into the world in Hayward, California on the 2nd of May, 1972 to parents Ata and Rocky Johnson. Dwayne was born into a professional wrestling dynasty. Dwayne's maternal grandfather, Peter "High Chief" Maivia, was a professional wrestler in the 1960s and 1970s. Peter Maivia was of Polynesian, specifically Samoan descent and had ties to the Anoa'i family. This connection to the Anoa'i family means that Dwayne is a cousin to other famous wrestlers such as Yokozuna, Rikishi, Roman Reigns, Umaga and Rosey. Dwayne's maternal grandmother, Lia Maivia, was a wrestling promoter.

Dwayne's father, Rocky "Soulman" Johnson was a black Canadian from Nova Scotia. Rocky Johnson was a professional wrestler and boxer. He was George Foreman's sparring partner in 1974 as Foreman prepared for "The Rumble in the Jungle" with legendary boxer Muhammad Ali. Peter "High Chief" Maivia and Rocky "Soulman" Johnson met on the wrestling circuit and became friends. At one time, Peter Maivia invited Rocky Johnson to his home, where Johnson met and fell in love with Maivia's daughter, Ata. The love between the two blossomed and they eventually married. Shortly after, Dwayne Douglas Johnson was born. His parents' Nova Scotian and Samoan ancestry explain Dwayne Johnson's exotic looks.

From a very young age, Dwayne Johnson grew up watching his father take on other wrestlers in the ring. Due to his father's wrestling career, Johnson grew up all over the country. During his early years, he briefly lived with his mother's family in New Zealand, where he attended Richmond Road Primary School. He later joined his parents in the United States and moved around with them as his father moved across different cities according to the demands of his wrestling career. By the time he was in his early teens, Dwayne had lived in thirty-eight states. As a result of the constant moving, young Dwayne did not learn how to make friends easily. His first true love was going on the road with his dad. From the age of five, he would accompany his dad to the gym, and although his dad never allowed him to lift weights, Dwayne developed a love affair with the gym that runs strong to this day.

Dwayne was physically imposing from a very young age. He was bigger than most kids his age. Since he did not have many friends, other children viewed him as a socially awkward kid and started teasing him, both for his big size and his father's choice of career. Because of this, Johnson developed a quick temper, and got into the habit of getting into fights with other children from a very young age.

When he was eight years old, Dwayne started taking part in sports at school, trying several sporting activities, including soccer, baseball, gymnastics and martial arts. Due to his huge physique and athleticism, he was very good in most of these sports. However, he was not really passionate about any of them. What he wanted to do was to hit the gym and pump iron. Unfortunately, his father felt that he was not ready yet. He would have to wait until he was thirteen before his father allowed him to truly enter the gym.

During his teens, the frequent moves that his father's career demanded slowed down, and the family settled in Bethlehem, Pennsylvania. Here, Dwayne joined Freedom High School. By this time, Dwayne was really good in the gym and had grown very big, standing at 6 feet 3 inches tall. When he started at Freedom High School, some students even mistook him for an undercover cop who was out to sting students using drugs. Due to his huge size, Dwayne became very cocky. His only real passion at the time was hitting the gym. Whenever he was away from the gym, he always seemed to find himself in trouble, or rather, trouble had a way of finding him. This was compounded by the fact that his father was rarely at home to give him a sense of direction.

Even though his father was still a force to be reckoned with in the wrestling circuits, his success inside the ring did not translate to financial success. The family was nowhere near any kind of financial stability. At the time, the Johnsons were living in an efficiency apartment that cost $120 a week. They went through a series of financial misfortunes which saw Dwayne's mother's car repossessed. A short while after, unable to pay the rent for their efficiency apartment, the family was evicted. The eviction took such a huge toll on the family that Dwayne's mother tried to commit suicide by walking into traffic. Young Dwayne had to rush into the traffic and wrestle his mother to the ground to keep her from being run over by oncoming cars. Seeing his family going through such financial woes was so difficult at this time for Dwayne that he started spiraling into depression. However, it also showed him how precious life is and how it can end in a matter of seconds.

The bouts of depression coupled with the pain of seeing his family struggling with basic needs would lead Dwayne Johnson down a treacherous path. He joined a group of other unruly teenagers who would target and rob tourists shopping in the high end shopping malls of Waikiki, all in a bid to chip in something to the family. However, his days as part of the theft ring were numbered. Soon after, he was arrested for theft. He would go on to be arrested eight more times. His final brush with the law came when he was caught up in a check fraud incident. He was fifteen years old at the time. When his parents came to pick him up from the police station, he saw the pain in his mother's eyes and realized that he was causing his parents bigger trouble than their financial woes. He vowed to himself that day that he would never trouble his parents again.

While the vow he made to himself kept Dwayne from going back to the theft ring, it did not keep him from trouble. The next day after being released from police custody, he went to school and got into an altercation with another kid. Dwayne knocked the kid out cold, resulting in a two-week suspension from school. After returning to school from suspension, he decided that the student's bathrooms were smelly, and, unable to put up with the smell, he walked through the teacher's lounge and into the teacher's bathrooms. Just as he was washing his hands after finishing his business, a short, barrel-chested teacher named Jody Cwik walked in on him and asked him to leave. Johnson turned, looked at the teacher and told him that he would leave when he was done, then turned back to continue washing his hands.

When he went home that night, he sat in bed and

pondered the events of the day. He realized that he had behaved rudely towards the teacher, and made a decision to make things right between him and the teacher. After getting to school the next morning, he found the class where Jody was teaching and walked in. He held out his hand and gave his apology for his behavior the previous day. Jody accepted Johnson's apology and then said something that would have a profound impact on Johnson's life: "I want you to play football for me."

Jody was the football coach at Freedom High, and he saw potential in the big bodied teen. Dwayne Johnson joined the football team and became very passionate about the game. It provided him with a constructive activity to channel his energy into, and gave him a sense of direction. Jody was a great coach who focused not only on his students' performance on the gridiron, but also in class. He guided Johnson to become not only a better football player, but also a better performer in class and a well-behaved student in general.

Johnson soon realized that football could provide him with a ticket out of the financial problems that his family was going through. He put all his focus in the sport, determined to earn himself a scholarship and become the first member of the Maivia family to go to college. He became so good at football that in his senior year at Freedom High, he made it to USA Today's High School All-American Team as one of the best defensive tackles in the USA. His determination to excel at football paid off. By the time he graduated from Freedom High, he had received offers from several colleges. Dwayne decided to join the University of Miami on full scholarship, where he joined the football team as a defensive tackle.

At University of Miami, his strength, size and determination made him a great player, and he was picked to be part of the Miami Hurricanes' national championship team; the first freshman to ever be picked in the team. Everything seemed to be going so well for Johnson, until disaster struck! One day, during practice, Johnson had an injury, dislocating his shoulder and tearing a number of ligaments. He was taken to hospital where the doctors performed some reconstructive surgery on his shoulder, before delivering some terrible news: his shoulder would need about one year to recover fully. That meant a full year without playing football. Johnson was out of the team just as the season was about to begin.

On hearing that it would take a year before he could play again, Dwayne was crushed. He slipped into depression once again. He stopped attending his classes. After a few weeks of living in depression, he decided to pack his things and return home. He stayed home for about two weeks, until the Miami

Hurricanes' head coach gave him a call and said he wanted to meet with him.

Once again, it would take a football coach to turn around the life of Dwayne Johnson, which seemed to be headed for destruction. When Johnson went back to Miami, the Miami Hurricanes' head coach was mad. He gave Johnson a talk down, telling him that he had greatly disappointed the team by behaving as he had done. The head coach gave Johnson an ultimatum. He would require Johnson to attend every class, get the signature of each teacher to show that he had attended each class that day, and then come to practice each day, even if he would have to sit on the sidelines due to his injury. Failure to do so would resort in his scholarship being cancelled.

Dwayne thought deeply about his life and decided that if he wanted to achieve anything, he would need to face and overcome the challenges he was facing. He had to follow the order of the Miami Hurricanes' head coach. With the help of Dany Garcia, his then-girlfriend who would also become his future wife, Johnson regained control over his life. He started excelling academically, and was even appointed as the academic captain. In 1995, Dwayne graduated from the University of Miami with a Bachelor's degree in criminology and psychology, and a 2.9 GPA.

When he joined the University of Miami, Johnson's dream was to become a National Football League (NFL) player. However, after a year on the sidelines due to injury, Johnson's performance on the gridiron took a hit. He was not as nimble on his feet as he was before the injury. As a result, he missed out on the chance to play for an NFL team. However, Johnson was still passionate about football, and when he received an offer from the Calgary Stampeders, a Canadian team, he took the offer and went to Calgary as a practice squad player.

Unfortunately for Dwayne, life in Canada was not as easy as he had anticipated. He was rarely getting any game time at the Stampeders. The weekly salary was less than $200. The salary was only enough for a small apartment in the outskirts of Calgary. Unable to buy a bed for himself, he found a mattress in a dumpster and took it to his apartment. Buying food was next to impossible, so he started all the Stampeder meetings so that he could get the free sandwiches that were served during the meetings. Despite the hardships, Johnson was determined to stay at the Calgary Stampeders and make things work. However, luck was not on his side. When the Stampeders got the chance to sign a former NFL player, they decided to let Johnson go, just two months after he had moved to Canada.

Getting cut from the Stampeders crushed Johnson once

again. He was 22 years old when he was cut from the team. At a time when his former teammates at Miami Hurricanes were signing multi-million dollar contracts with NFL teams, Johnson's career as a football player was effectively over. For someone who had spent the last ten years dreaming of becoming a professional football player, this was a huge blow. He became depressed, spending all his time watching TV and sulking in his room. This time, however, it wouldn't take another football coach to get his life back on track, but rather his own initiative. After two weeks of sulking in his room, something clicked in his mind, and he came to the realization that he would have to face his failures and setbacks by himself. With only seven bucks between him and poverty, Johnson made a decision that has become one of his most famous quotes. He came to the realization that he was broke as hell, and he vowed to himself that he would change his fate:

"In 1995 I had $7 bucks in my pocket and knew two things: I'm broke as hell and one day I won't be."

Ever since he first stepped on the gridiron, Dwayne Johnson had developed a very specific vision for his future. According to his vision, Johnson would become the next Michael Strahan. He saw himself winning the Super Bowl, having a big mansion in New Jersey and marrying a beautiful wife. However, being cut off from the Stampeders threatened this future he had envisioned. At that point, a fire was lit in Johnson's heart. He decided that even though he could no longer achieve his vision through football, he had to find another way to achieve it. After a short while, the Calgary Stampeders' head coach gave Johnson a call and gave him another chance to try out for the Stampeders. However, Johnson had made a decision that football was no longer the thing for him. Instead, he decided to join the family business – wrestling.

Chapter Two: The Family Business

"When life puts you in touchy situations, don't say "Why Me?" Just say "Try Me."" – Dwayne Johnson

After hitting rock bottom in Canada and making the decision to quit his dream of becoming a professional football player, Dwayne Johnson flew back to his parents' home in Tampa. Once he got home, he told his parents that he had quit football and now wanted to try his hand at wrestling. His mother and his girlfriend were very supportive of his decision and encouraged him to give it a shot. When he approached his father asking him to be his trainer, it did not go quite as he had expected. Having spent his entire life as a wrestler, Dwayne Johnson's father knew that the life of a professional wrestler was not easy, and he did not want his son to go through the same tough life he had gone through. He told his son that getting into wrestling could end up being the biggest mistake he will ever make.

However, Dwayne would not be put off. He kept pleading

with his father to train him. Finally, his father gave in and agreed to train Dwayne on one condition – Dwayne had to put in 110% effort towards the training. Dwayne, who had grown up seeing other wrestlers putting in hard work at the gym knew that this was something he was ready to do. With the condition accepted, Rocky Johnson put his son on a grueling training regimen. The training Rocky put Dwayne through was more than physical. Rocky also taught his son how to be a showman, how to work the crowds. After training for several months, Rocky felt confident that Dwayne could now step into the ring and take on other wrestlers.

Rocky reached out to Pat Patterson, a former wrestler who had become a talent agent and asked him to help Dwayne Johnson get into - what was then called - the WWF or World Wrestling Federation. After watching Dwayne take on other wrestlers in amateur competitions, Patterson saw potential in the young man, and about a year after being cut off by the Calgary Stampeders, Dwayne Johnson made his debut into the WWF, with Patterson's help. He could not buy himself wrestling trunks, boots or knee pads. Instead, he had to borrow these from one of his uncles.

Despite signing with Patterson's help, Dwayne Johnson did not start in the major league. He started his wrestling career in Memphis in the United States Wrestling Alliance, the

WWF's second tier league. Here, Dwayne, who was using the name Flex Kavana, used to earn between $20 and $40 per match. However, Dwayne was determined to make wrestling work for him, and he gave it his all. After a match with a famous wrestler known as Owen Hart, Dwayne Johnson impressed his promoters so much that he was transferred to the WWF headquarters in Connecticut. On November 16 1996, Dwayne made his first appearance in a big match at Madison Square Gardens in New York City, using the name "Rocky Maivia" as a tribute to his father Rocky Johnson and Grandfather Peter Maivia.

The WWF event where Rocky Maivia made his maiden appearance was known as the Survivor's Series. During this event, Rocky Maivia was presented as a "good guy", or a "baby face" in wrestling lingo. Once again, Dwayne did not disappoint. He went on to become the last man standing in the event, against "bad guys" or "heels" like Paul Levesque, better known by his stage name, Triple H. By emerging as the last man standing in the Survivor Series, Dwayne Johnson made his mark immediately in the WWF.

Ever since his debut at the Survivor Series, Rocky Maivia was marketed as a good guy or baby face. With his huge size, incredible speed, and his charm on the microphone, Rocky Maivia quickly became a favorite with the crowds. In

February 1997, just a few months into his professional wrestling career, Dwayne Johnson won his first WWF Intercontinental Championship. Dwayne was 24 years old at the time, making him the youngest wrestler to ever win the title. From there, he went on to defend the title three times in quick succession. However, instead of endearing him to the crowds even more, the combination of his success in the ring, his cheesy character and his good guy persona led to rejection by WWF fans. Fans started becoming hostile towards him, booing him during matches and raising signs written "Rocky Sucks" and "Die Rocky, Die". Fans were more interested in the bad guys or heels, instead of this good guy who was winning matches left, right and center. If Dwayne Johnson was to survive in wrestling, he would need to come up with a new strategy.

Later in 1997, Dwayne was forced to take a break from the ring due to a knee injury. During this break, Dwayne got married to his college sweetheart, Dany Garcia. He also took this time to think up a new strategy that would make him a crowd favorite once again. By now, the wrestling industry had evolved greatly. WWF promoters had realized that there was a lot of money to be made in wrestling. As a result, wrestling had transformed from the athletic sport that his father and grandfather had engaged in into showbiz. It was all about working the crowds. Matches were now being choreographed and the winners determined even before the actual match. Dwayne Johnson realized that if he was to remain relevant in the wrestling industry, he would need to come up with a new persona for his exploits in the ring. Working with the help of WWF writers and producers, Dwayne came up with a new persona that would take his success in the ring to new heights.

After his injury, Dwayne Johnson returned to wrestling as The Rock, a badass character who would become a force to reckon with in WWF. As part of the transformation, The Rock got a huge tattoo of a Brahma bull on his left shoulder and bicep. He also joined the "Nation of Domination", a group of bad boy wrestlers that included wrestlers like Kama, D'Lo Brown and Faarooq. He transformed his charm on the mic into menacing tough talk that he would use to threaten his opponents before crushing them in the ring. He also developed the habit of talking about himself in third person. After the transformation, the WWF audience fell in love with The Rock, and were always looking forward to watching him take on opponents, both in the press and in the ring.

Under his new persona, Dwayne Johnson became a very formidable opponent inside the ring, causing a lot of trouble for experienced wrestling superstars such as Triple H, "Stone Cold" Steve Austin and Mankind. To keep up the hype, WWF producers created grudges between The Rock and several other wrestling superstars, with The Rock winning the mock grudge matches, losing, and then winning again. At some point, The Rock realized that he was better off on his own instead of remaining as part of the "Nation of Domination". He left the group, which collapsed after he left.

The Rock became a regular holder of the WWF Championship belt. In 1999, The Rock and Mankind had several fights against each other, during which the WWF Championship belt was exchanged between the two of them a number of times. Towards the end of the year, the two joined hands to create a team that was referred to as the Rock 'n Sock Connection. As a team, the Rock and Mankind won the tag team championships thrice. They also performed a number of comedy skits together. One of the most popular ones was known as "This Is Your Life", which aired on Raw Is War. The show, which earned an 8.4 Nielsen rating, featured people from The Rock's past, including Jody Cwik, his high school football coach and his high school girlfriend.

Though The Rock had come back as a villain, his amusing skills on the mic and entertaining promos led to so much popularity for him that he labeled himself "The People's Champion". The Rock would go on to become the poster boy for WWF for the better part of the following decade, during which he was labeled the most popular wrestler ever in the history of the WWF. The WWF fraternity was quick to take advantage of The Rock's popularity and turn it into financial returns. The Rock's brand became a major income earner for the WWF. T-shirts, Halloween Masks and posters were made and sold in the millions. Video games and action figures were created around The Rock's character. During The Rock's prime as a professional wrestler, the WWF was making over 120 million dollars every year from sales of The Rock merchandise.

The Rock's popularity was not restricted to hardcore wrestling fans. Due to Dwayne Johnson's exotic movie star looks, his popularity caught on with women. During his prime, The Rock is said to have doubled the number of female fans watching the WWF. In the year 2000, The Rock published his first autobiography. In testimony to his popularity, the autobiography became a New York Times Bestseller and remained in the bestseller list for almost half a year, which is quite an achievement. In a bid to promote his book, The Rock started appearing on Television. These TV appearances made The Rock start thinking about moving from wrestling to taking up roles in films.

The Rock also main evented WrestleMania 29, which had the second highest attendance numbers in the history of the

WWF. His return to wrestling in 2001 led to the show's highest rating for that year. His steel cage match against Shane McMahon became the most viewed professional wrestling match in the history of the WWF, which changed its acronym around 2002 to WWE after a court case to stop any legal confusion with the international wildlife charity, World Wide Fund for Nature.

After his match against McMahon, The Rock received an indefinite suspension from wrestling. However, this suspension would not be the end of his wrestling career. In January 2003, The Rock was back in the ring. Before his return, he had spent some considerable time insulting Hulk Hogan. After a huge build up, The Rock and Hulk Hogan had a fight where The Rock cemented his wrestling prowess by defeating Hulk Hogan. He also started performing his famous "Rock Concerts", where he performed with a guitar while ridiculing and taunting the city hosting the match.

Later, The Rock attempted to win the World Heavyweight Championship. However, his attempt was not successful. In retaliation for his loss, The Rock started a feud with wrestler "Stone Cold" Steve Austin, who had recently been named as the superstar of the decade. To make matters worse, The Rock and Austin had previously met at WrestleMania, with Austin winning the two matches. After a buildup that involved a lot of taunting and name calling, the two eventually had a fight at WrestleMania XIX, where the Rock won. Following the win, WWE held an event dubbed "The Rock Appreciation Night" to celebrate The Rock's win. However, during the event, a debuting wrestler known as Goldberg attacked The Rock. The Rock and Goldberg had a match at Backlash, during which The Rock lost. After the loss, The Rock took another break from active wrestling.

However, The Rock still kept coming back to WWE sporadically. In 2011, he was brought back as the host of that year's WrestleMania. During this time, The Rock developed a feud with John Cena, one that would go on for the next two years. The Rock would also be involved in non-wrestling roles throughout this time. In 2016, Dwayne "The Rock" Johnson finally retired from his wrestling career. By this time, he had built a name for himself as one of the greatest pro wrestlers in the history of the sport. He had made a record by becoming the first person ever to win the WWE championship six times, and then extended the record by winning it seven times. He also held the intercontinental championship for 265 days, longer than any other wrestler in the modern era.

By the time he retired from wrestling, The Rock had also earned the respect of his fellow wrestlers. Hulk Hogan, despite also being one of the pro wrestling greats, referred to

The Rock as the biggest wrestling superstar. John Cena, a 16 time WWE champion echoed Hulk Hogan's sentiments, terming The Rock as the biggest superstar in the history of WWE. In the book *"The WrestleCrap Book of Lists"*, R. D. Reynolds also referred to The Rock as the biggest wrestling superstar between 1999 and 2004. The same sentiment has also been echoed by other wrestling greats like Chris Jericho and Ric Flair.

The Rock's popularity in the wrestling universe also had a lot of influence in WWE. One of WWE's longest running TV series, Smackdown, was derived from one of The Rock's most popular catch phrases – 'lay the smackdown". The Rock was also the main star in WrestleMania XXVIII, which is recorded as having the highest number of pay-per-view subscribers worldwide in the history of the WWE. He was also the main attraction at WrestleMania X-Seven, which holds the record of having the highest number of pay-per-view customers in the United States.

Despite achieving so much success within the wrestling industry, and dominating the wrestling headlines for close to a decade, The Rock was not satisfied. He wanted more. While promoting his autobiography on TV, The Rock had already started thinking about crossing over to film. Having already won everything there was to win in WWE, The Rock decided to transfer his charm, good looks and tough talk to the silver screen.

Chapter Three: Conquering The Big Screen

"My work, my goal, my life, it's like a treadmill. And there's no stop-button on my treadmill. Once I get on, I just keep going." – Dwayne Johnson

The Rock's prowess in the ring combined with his cocky interviews and story lines made his popularity cross over from wrestling fans to the mainstream media. In 2000, The Rock's popularity in mainstream media increased when he made a guest appearance on the music video for hip hop track "It Doesn't Matter" by Wyclef Jean. While still an active WWE wrestler, Dwayne also started hosting Saturday Night Live, a popular sketch comedy TV series. The TV series became very popular with viewers, and it greatly helped to demonstrate The Rock's comedic ability and acting prowess.

Shortly after, several Hollywood directors started approaching The Rock with the aim of featuring him in their projects. This was the beginning of The Rock's foray into film, which would see him become one of the most successful and highest paid actors in Hollywood. The Rock would create the

Seven Bucks Productions, a film production company, together with his ex-wife and her brother. The Rock chose the name Seven Bucks as a tribute to his lowly moment in Canada when he only had seven bucks between him and poverty. Over the course of his acting career, Dwayne Johnson also dropped the stage name "The Rock" and chose to be known by his given name.

Dwayne began his journey into film in 1999 by playing a role in one episode of a popular television show known as the *That '70s Show*. The show had an episode titled "That Wrestling Show", in which Dwayne Johnson played his own father. The show was a success, and it helped paint his acting capabilities in even better light. In 2000, a year after appearing on "That Wrestling Show", Dwayne appeared in an episode of *Star Trek: Voyager*. In the episode titled "Tsunkatse", Dwayne played the role of an alien wrestler who was pitted against a popular character known as Seven of Nine.

Johnson played his first major role in a major film in 2001, shortly after being suspended indefinitely from WWE. He played the role of the Scorpion King in the movie *The Mummy Returns*. The movie was a great success, earning a gross profit of $335 million. It also earned Dwayne Johnson the Teen Choice Award of the Choice Movie Villain, despite his appearance in the movie being limited. Owing to his performance in the movie, another movie was created as a reprisal of his role. In the new movie, titled *The Scorpion King*, Dwayne was given a leading role, his first ever leading role in a movie. For his role in *The Scorpion King*, he earned a whopping $5.5 million, thereby etching his name in the Guinness Book of Records as the highest paid debut actor.

With a more prominent role in *The Scorpion King*, Dwayne established himself as someone who was destined to be a movie star. With the success of his first two movies, the offers started coming in hard and fast for the newest kid in Hollywood. Soon after, in 2003, Dwayne starred in the movie *The Rundown*, a comedic action movie in which he played the role of a bounty hunter sent to Brazil by his employer to retrieve the employer's son. In 2004, Dwayne starred in the movie *Walking Tall*, a remake of a 1973 action movie by the same name. Once again, *Walking Tall* was a success, and helped Johnson enhance his suitability for the role of a tough action hero.

He continued to feature in several movies, one after the other, and sometimes several movies concurrently. In 2005, he put his comedic prowess at use by playing a supporting role in *Be Cool*, together with actors Uma Thurman and John Travolta. In a bid to look more like a movie star and less than a wrestler, Dwayne also underwent plastic surgery to reduce the size of his pectoral muscles. In 2006, Dwayne co-starred with Karl Urban and Rosamund Pike in *Doom*, a science fiction action horror movie in which he played the role of the primary antagonist. In the following years, Dwayne continued appearing in movies, switching between action films and comedy flicks. He appeared in the movies *Gridiron Gang, Reno 911!: Miami, Southland Tales, The Game Plan* and *Get Smart*. In 2008, in his role as Joe Kingman in *The Game Plan*, Dwayne received a nomination for Favorite Movie Actor at the Nickelodeon's Kids Choice Awards. However, Dwayne Johnson did not win the award, which went to Johnny Depp for his role in *Pirates of the Caribbean: At World's End*. Dwayne's film acting career was accompanied by various TV show appearances. In 2009, Dwayne was featured in episodes of Wizards of Waverly Place and Cory in the House. He also hosted the 2009 Nickelodeon Kids Choice Awards.

With Dwayne Johnson's popularity as an actor spreading, fans started demanding to see a head to head face-off between Dwayne and Vin Diesel, the lead star in the very popular *Fast and Furious* franchise. This led to Dwayne appearing in the fifth *Fast and Furious* movie, playing the role of a tough cop known as Luke Hobbs. In *The Fast and Furious*, Dwayne finally found a franchise where he truly felt at home - one that helped him cement his position as one of the best actors today. He also got a chance to work with Vin Diesel - something that he had been looking forward to. The fifth installment of the *Fast and Furious* franchise turned out to be a great success, grossing over $86 million in profit during its opening weekend, and $676 million total. To this day, no other Dwayne Johnson movie has had such a huge opening. Appearing on *Fast Five* also provided Dwayne with the opportunity to work with Universal Studios once again, the first studio he worked with when starting his acting career. From there, Dwayne, in his role as Luke Hobbs, became a natural part in the *Fast and Furious* franchise. In 2013, he appeared in the sequel *Fast and Furious 6*. From there, he has been involved in all the *Fast and Furious* movies, playing a central role in *Fast and Furious 7* and *Fast and Furious 8*. After a feud with fellow *Fast and Furious* co-star Vin Diesel, it is not very clear whether Dwayne will appear in *Fast and Furious 9*, which is expected to hit the studios in 2020. In an interview, Dwayne said he would only appear on the film if he and Vin Diesel were able to sort out their differences. There has also been talk of a Fast and Furious spin-off, titled *Hobbs & Shaw*, which will focus on the characters of Luke Hobbs and Deckard Shaw, the latter played by Jason Statham. The spinoff is scheduled to be released in 2019.

In 2013, Dwayne also appeared in *G.I. Joe: Retaliation*, a

military sci-fi action movie. By this time, he had already created a name for himself as a bankable movie star whose inclusion in a film equated with success for the film. His role in invigorating the *G.I. Joe* and *Fast and Furious* franchises even earned him a special nickname – "The Franchise Viagra". 2013 also saw Dwayne star in a number of true story movies, including *Pain and Gain* and *Empire State.* Dwayne also hosted and produced *The Hero,* a TNT reality competition series. He also won the 2013 Nickelodeon Kids Choice Awards for the Favorite Male Buttkicker. In the same year, he also announced that he would be producing and starring in an HBO TV series titled *Ballers,* a comedy drama series which would be based on the lives of professional football players in Miami. 2013 was a great year for Dwayne Johnson. By the end of the year, he had earned $1.3 billion from his acting, and in December he was listed by Forbes magazine as the highest earning actor of the year. According to Forbes, *Fast and Furious 6,* which grossed $789 million worldwide, played a huge role in helping him become the highest earning actor of the year.

In 2014, Dwayne played the lead role in *Hercules*, a 3D action fantasy adventure movie. To play the role of Hercules, Dwayne had to double his workout and nutrition routine, since the movie required him to be as muscular as possible. The movie was a success, grossing $244 million worldwide.

While the movie received mixed reviews overall, Dwayne's acting in the movie was widely praised. In 2014, Dwayne also hosted *Wake Up Call,* another TBT reality series. He also announced that he would be producing Seal Team 666, a horror movie.

In June 2015, the first episode of *Ballers* aired. In the series, Dwayne Johnson plays the role of a retired professional football player who transitions into a career as a financial manager for other professional football players. The series was a huge success. The series is currently in its third season, with the fourth season set to premier in August 2018. Before the release of the first season of *Ballers,* there was a risk that Dwayne would end up being confined to films that required him to play the role of a mean, tough guy in action scenes. However, his role in *Ballers* showed that he could express his talents really well in films that are not action oriented. In the same year, Dwayne also starred in *San Andreas,* a disaster movie written by Carlton Cuse.

2016 was another great year for Dwayne Johnson. Once again getting in touch with his humorous side, Johnson teamed up with his buddy Kevin Hart to star in *Central Intelligence,* an action comedy movie where Johnson and Kevin play the roles of two old high school buddies who have to team up to save the world from a terror threat. *Central*

Intelligence also turned out to be a great success. The movie brought in $127 million in Northern America, making it the highest grossing domestic comedy for 2016. In the same year, Dwayne was also picked to play the lead voice role in *Moana*, a Disney animated film in which he voices Maui, a legendary demigod who also displays the signature eyebrow raise that was part of Dwayne Johnson's trademark in the WWE. Dwayne closed the year by being named as the: "Sexiest Man Alive" by the People Magazine, replacing David Beckham, the British soccer player.

In 2017, Johnson also appeared in *Baywatch*, co-starring alongside Zac Efron. *Baywatch* was a classic beach and babes comedic action film that is adapted from a TV series by the same name. However, *Baywatch* did not live up to its hype. It only grossed $177 million internationally and received several "Golden Raspberry" nominations. 2017 also saw Dwayne appear in *The Fate of the Furious* once again as Luke Hobbs. He also teamed up with Kevin Hart once again as the co-star in *Jumanji: Welcome to the Jungle*, a sequel to a 1995 movie by the same name. Jumanji was a huge hit with fans, bringing in $829 million so far. Dwayne Johnson and Kevin Hart are now working on a third sequel for the movie, set to be released in 2019.

2018 also looks like a promising year for Dwayne Johnson,

with movies such as *Rampage* hitting the theatres. *Rampage* is a film about a troop of monsters that wreak havoc on cities while armed forces are deployed in an attempt to stop the monsters. Before getting on set for *Rampage*, Dwayne had an argument with the movie's directors because he did not want a sad ending for the movie. According to Johnson, the brand he has built for himself requires that his audience are left feeling good after watching a movie he is involved in. He was even ready to step away from the movie, forcing the directors to come up with a compromise that would leave his audience feeling uplifted. Such is the kind of seriousness that Dwayne puts into his work. However, his gut feeling was not wrong. After its premier, *Rampage* grossed $154 million in China and $97 in the United States, making it one of the top 20 highest grossing international movies in China. Dwayne has also been producing a seriocomedy titled *Fighting With My Family*, in which he is also set to play a critical role. In February 2018, during the flurry of advertising that goes along with the Super Bowl, Dwayne debuted a trailer for *Skyscraper*, an action movie set to premier in 2018 in which he plays the role of a former FBI agent and amputee who has to save his family from a skyscraper which is on fire.

Aside from the above movies, there are several other films where Dwayne Johnson is expected to play the role of the lead actor. Already, filmmaker Shane Black as gotten into an agreement with Dwayne that will see Johnson play the role of "Doc" in Doc Savage, a guy that was mentally and physically trained from birth to become the perfect human specimen. Doc has heightened senses, the perfect body and genius-level intellect. Dwayne has expressed a lot of enthusiasm for the movie, which is set to be backed by Original Film and Sony Pictures. Filming for Doc Savage is likely to start later in 2018.

After the success of *San Andreas,* which grossed $473 million worldwide, Dwayne Johnson will also be joining with producer Beau Flynn and director Brad Peyton to come up with a sequel for the movie, which will be titled *San Andreas 2.* While no release date or trailer has been issued for the sequel, you can expect the same gripping action that has become synonymous with Dwayne Johnson. He will also play a central role in *Big Trouble In Little China,* a remake of the 1986 classic of the same name by John Carpenter. Not only will Dwayne be acting in it, he will also be involved in the production of the film, with the backing of 20th Century Fox.

Dwayne Johnson has also been associated with *Alpha Squad Seven,* a science fiction comedy action movie that is set in space. The film is expected to expand into a franchise, which does not come as a surprise when you consider that Dwayne is set to play a leading role in the film. In the film,

Dwayne will co-star alongside an unannounced actor. Johnson and director Brad Peyton are also possibly going to reunite for a film titled *Journey 3: From The Earth To The Moon*. The film had been set for a June 2017 release date, which was later postponed indefinitely.

Universal Studios and James Vanderbilt are also working on a plan to create a series of films adapting the *Paul Janson* book series - written by Robert Ludlum, creator of the *Bourne* franchise - into a cinematic universe, starting with a movie titled *The Janson Directive*. Dwayne is set to play the role of Paul Janson, the ex-Navy SEAL who is the main protagonist in Ludlum's book, which is also named *The Janson Directive*. As part of the cinematic universe, other Ludlum movies that will be adapted into films include *Covert One, The Sigma Protocol* and *The Parsifal Mosaic*. With such a series of movies in line, it is expected that Dwayne will have a lot more work coming, provided that he plays his role in *The Janson Directive* successfully, which is more than likely.

There are plans by Disney to turn the Disneyland Jungle Cruise ride into a film, following the path that was set by *Pirates of the Caribbean*. There have been rumors associating Dwayne with the film, though he is yet to confirm the rumors himself. Johnson will also play the role of Black Adam in the DC/Warner Bros comic project titled *Shazam*. The film is set to be released in 2019. Johnson is also set to play the role of a producer in Sony's film adaptation of Jay Longino's graphic novel titled *Son of Shaolin*. Dwayne is set to be involved in other films like *The Rundown 2, G.I Joe 3* and *Wolf Man*.

By quitting football in favor of wrestling, and later on transitioning his fame inside the ring into an acting career, Dwayne Johnson has been able to achieve the vision he had as a teenager playing football for the Miami Hurricanes. While he did not win the Super Bowl, he has won numerous accolades as a wrestler and an actor and managed to buy a 13,000 square foot mansion in South Florida.

After he had become a movie star, Dwayne once bumped into Michael Strahan, his teenage idol. When Johnson mentioned that he used to fantasize about being Michael Strahan, Strahan was genuinely flattered, saying he wouldn't mind trading lives with the man Dwayne Johnson had become.

So far, at the age of 46 years, Dwayne Johnson has achieved more success than he ever envisioned, more than he would ever have achieved as a professional football player. His success has been driven by a number of factors: First and foremost is his charisma. Ever since his childhood, he has been a consummate showman, electrifying the room with his charm and stage presence. Despite his success and public life,

Dwayne is also a very humble individual. Without the charisma and humility, it would have been very difficult for him to transition from a debutante wrestler into the megastar he is today.

In addition, Dwayne has always been very competitive. From his football days, to his wrestling days, to acting, everything to him is about winning. He has a deep drive to win, and will do anything it takes to win. He is also very entertaining, something that proved crucial for him in his wrestling and acting careers. He always finds a way to get the audience involved in his performance. Like he says, his audience are his employers, and he does everything to make sure they get what they expect of him, which is to be entertained. Finally, Dwayne Johnson is a very hard worker. Whether in the gym or in a movie set, he is always the hardest worker in the room. For instance, during the set of *Pain and Gain*, he had to put on fifteen pounds of muscle, something that required him to increase his workout and nutrition regime significantly. During the set of the film, Johnson and co-star Mark Wahlberg were eating a staggering seventeen meals every single day.

Chapter Four: Rules for Success

"Think back five years ago. Think of where you're at today. Think ahead five years and what you want to accomplish. Be unstoppable." - Dwayne Johnson.

Rule One: Be Yourself

One of Dwayne's most important rules for success is to be himself. Early in his wrestling career, Dwayne - then known as 'Rocky' - endured taunts such as "Rocky sucks" from the fans. A tendon injury gave him a break from wrestling and time to reflect. He realized his unpopularity was from his attempt to be someone he wasn't. When he returned to wrestling, he embraced his true self and the fans loved his authenticity. He swapped the nickname 'Rocky' to the name he's famous for today - 'The Rock'.

In a digital world where things are not always what they seem, people value authenticity more than ever. Uniqueness is no longer a quality to hide; rather, it's a gift to grow, leverage, and celebrate. The path to your success starts by discovering your own identity, story, and way, and then follow it. Like The Rock, live your own truth and by your own rules.

Rule Two: Surround Yourself With the Right People

When Dwayne made the transition from wrestler to Hollywood actor, he knew that he needed to apply the same discipline to acting as he had to his previous work. What that meant was he needed to surround himself by people he could learn from and that would inspire him. He created a social circle of great acting coaches, experienced directors, and successful actors who all helped him to raise his game. He was humble enough to recognize that he didn't know everything about this field, but he was willing to spend time learning from the best.

It's said that you are the average of the five people you spend the most time with. Given this, who you choose to be close to has a major impact on your life. If you surround yourself with positive, happy people or people who inspire you to push yourself further, then you have a much better chance of succeeding.

Rule Three: Have Incredible Work Ethic

From an early age, Dwayne's father instilled a strong work ethic in Dwayne by exposing him to his strict workout routine. It taught him the importance of waking up, going after it, and putting in the work. This lesson continued into Dwayne's adult years. When he shoots a movie, he sleeps just five hours a night to give as much time as possible to his work responsibilities. Four hours before he has any morning appointments, he wakes up to to a cardio and weights workout and then has breakfast. He puts his other commitments first before himself.

Having strong work ethics helps you achieve your goals and gives you a sense of purpose to acknowledge things that are bigger than you. It's the drive to make your company a success, to get that promotion, or to live your passion. It builds trust and respect from those around you and puts you in a better position to receive more responsibility and grow.

Rule Four: Never Give Up

After Dwayne was cut from the Canadian Football League's Calgary Stampeders, he counted all the money he had - and it came to $7. At the same time, one of his co-players, Warren Sapp, had just been signed for millions of dollars. Success was all around him, but he wasn't getting any. However, he still had the drive to succeed and channeled his determination into wrestling and later into building a career in Hollywood. The fact he had no acting background didn't phase Dwayne and he sought out opportunities to develop the skills he needed to be an actor.

Believing in yourself is one of the key elements to success. It means being willing to accept failures and learn from them, rather than let them hold you back. As Dwayne knows, achieving your goals is not always easy and getting what you want depends on how much you are willing to work for it, against the odds.

Rule Five: Find Purpose

When he was 14 years-old, Dwayne saw his mom break down and cry after being evicted. He then vowed to never be homeless again and never see his mom cry again. Following the successful men he knew in his life, he swapped his two days per week training for intense, frequent sessions and focused on bodybuilding. This commitment to his goals went on to shape his entire future. It led him to be in a position where he could help his mom and didn't need to worry about being homeless again.

Your values will shape your sense of purpose and will determine your life goals. Having a sense of purpose is important as it's a key ingredient for having a meaningful and successful life. If you know what your goals are and why you want to achieve them, it will keep you motivated to pursue the things that truly matter to you.

Rule Six: Embrace Failure

Dwayne credits his past for making him who is today and once said, "it's undeniable that I'm a product of those tough times. I am a product of the most challenging times of my life." Despite being successful now, he's said that he still has the mindset of always being one week away from becoming homeless again and that is what keeps him pushing forward. Throughout his life, he has faced setbacks from football to embracing new worlds in wrestling and acting, yet these have been important parts of his personal and professional growth.

Failure is life's greatest teacher. Those who avoid it will make the same safe choices repeatedly and will always remain boxed into a comfort zone. To be successful and achieve big goals, you have to take risks and expect failure along the way. Whether you succeed or fail, you will learn so much about your strengths, determination, and talent.

Rule Seven: Just Bring It

One of Dwayne's most famous phrases is 'just bring it', a mantra he used during his WWE days. He would use it when he faced his opponents in the ring, yet it also represents his approach to his career and success. He never surrendered to a challenge in his career, whether it was wrestling or acting in a Hollywood movie. His day-to-day schedule is hectic with constant traveling, training, shooting films, and raising a family. Yet he still confronts any challenge fearlessly and pushes his boundaries.

Fear of the unknown or failure can hold us back. Yet if you face challenges, you can push past your mental barriers and achieve your goals of success. It makes you stronger, helps you understand your capabilities, and gives you space to learn and grow. When faced with a challenge, don't think that's your cue to give up. Do what The Rock does and face it head-on.

Rule Eight: Earn Respect

Dwayne once said, "Blood, sweat, and respect. First two you give. Last one you earn." The blood and sweat is the work you put in. The respect comes after and is something that is earned day after day. Dwayne started working out early and his relentless drive and commitment to bodybuilding earned him respect at his gym. Later in life, his strong work ethic and willingness to embrace challenges well outside his comfort zone made him well-respected in WWE and Hollywood.

Earning respect is all about how much you put into your work when no-one is watching. It's about throwing yourself into whatever it takes to fulfill your ambitions and not giving up when the going gets tough. Not everyone can do this, yet this is the difference between the average person and the world's most successful people. You also need to work hard at maintaining respect; once it's lost, it's not easy to get back.

Rule Nine: Be Persistent

Dwayne used to participate in sports as a kid, but his dad only allowed him to weight-lift when he was a teenager. On his first day, he tried to bench press with heavy weights, but couldn't lift them. However, it made him more determined to be able to. He started training as much as he could, applying the same work ethic he had seen his dad and other wrestlers show. His efforts paid off and he eventually managed to lift it. Being persistent has been an important part of Dwayne's success from football and wrestling to his Hollywood career.

Persistent is the ability to keep on going, even when things get difficult. It's about not quitting when you suffer a setback. It's about learning the lesson of failure and keep on going. Those who are able to be persistent have more chance of achieving their goals and being successful.

Rule Ten: Learn to Listen

As Dwayne once said, "know your role and shut your mouth." He learned this valuable lesson from Iron Sheik, a world-renowned wrestler, who became a mentor to Dwayne and shared a lot of valuable knowledge and tips with him. Sheik once told him that if he was to be good in the business of wrestling, he would have to learn to keep quiet and keep his ears open. It was advice that Dwayne applied everywhere from the wrestling locker room to the Hollywood film sets.

An ability to listen is vital for good communication and to understand the mind and desires of the other person. Being successful in life involves your interactions with others and so being able to communicate properly is an essential skill to learn. This means replacing talking with active listening in order to remain open to new ideas and build better relationships with others.

Chapter Five: Personal Life

"One of the most important things you can accomplish is just being yourself." –
Dwayne Johnson

From his humble beginnings as the first son of a modest professional wrestler who hustled wrestling matches to provide for his parents and siblings, Dwayne Johnson has established himself as one of the most successful actors of the 21st century. He has also established himself as the de facto alpha male persona in the mainstream entertainment industry, becoming the people's champion in the film world just as he was in the world of wrestling. However, despite his popularity and fame, Dwayne keeps his private life very private, and very few people know Dwayne beyond what they see on the screen.

Here is what we know from public record: Dwayne Johnson has been married and divorced once. As told in the first chapter of the book, Johnson met his first wife Dany Garcia during his days as a student of the University of Miami. They developed a romantic relationship that lasted throughout their college days and early career. On May 3 1997, just a day after Dwayne Johnson's birthday, the two got married. Four years after their wedding, Dwayne Johnson and Dany Garcia welcomed a new member into the family. This was their daughter Simone Alexandra, who was born on the 14th of August 2001. Dwayne Johnson and Dany Garcia also created their production company, Seven Bucks Production, which they run together to this day.

However, due to some irreconcilable differences, Dwayne Johnson and Dany Garcia decided to split up on 1st June 2007 - ten years after they got married. Despite their split, the two vowed to stay friends, and have remained close to this day. Dany Garcia had been Dwayne Johnson's manager since the beginning of his career, and has helped Johnson create the image of himself that his fans know today. Despite their break-up, the two decided that Dany Garcia would continue managing Dwayne Johnson's career. While this would seem like an awkward set-up to "ordinary people", Dwayne and Dany are not "ordinary people". As if that is not enough, Dave Rienzi - Dany's new husband - serves as Dwayne Johnson's personal fitness trainer.

In 2006, while on the set for the movie *The Game Plan*, Dwayne met Lauren Hashian, a singer-songwriter and the daughter of Sib Hashian, the drummer for the famous rock band Boston. Shortly after the separation between Dwayne and his wife Dany, Johnson started dating Lauren Hashian. Though they are not officially married, the couple has been dating for more than a decade. In December 2015, Johnson and Lauren welcomed their first child, a daughter named Jasmine. In April 2018, came the arrival into the world of their second daughter, who they named Tiana Gia Johnson. Johnson and Lauren had planned to get married towards the end of 2017. However, the couple put the plans on hold after Lauren got pregnant with Tiana Gia. Dwayne Johnson's girlfriend and his ex-wife are on good terms, always appearing together for Johnson's movie premieres and celebrating holidays together with him.

In 2014, Dwayne Johnson, who has an estimated net worth of $220 million, bought a 13,700 square foot, $5.5 million home in Landmark Ranch Estates in Southwest Ranches, Florida. Immediately after paying for the house, he requested a $1 million extension be made to the house to include a gym and a guest house for his personal fitness trainer. Since the house was completed, Dwayne has been living there with his girlfriend, Lauren Hashian. Johnson also bought a house for his parents, fulfilling a dream that had been burning inside him ever since he saw his parents being evicted from their efficiency apartment during his teens. Dwayne is also a good friend to Arnold Schwarzenegger, the action movie star and former California Governor - the only other sportsman who made an equally successful crossover from the world of sports to the big screen.

Due to the connection to the Samoan Royal Chiefs, and in recognition to his service to the Samoan people, Dwayne Johnson was given the noble title of Seiuli by Malietoa Tanumafili II, the Samoan King. To keep touch with his Samoan roots, Dwayne has two Samoan tattoos, a Samoan pe'a tattoo and the tattoo of a bull's skull. Dwayne is also a dedicated supporter of the Samoan national rugby team.

Knowing the power and influence wielded by celebrities, Dwayne "The Rock" Johnson uses his popularity for public good. For instance, in the year 2000, he gave a speech at the Republican National Convention and attended the Democratic National Convention as part of the WWE's "Smackdown Your Vote" campaign, whose aim was to encourage young people to vote. In 2007, Dwayne and ex-wife Dany Garcia donated $1 million to the University of Miami towards the renovation of the university's football facility, making the donation the largest one ever to be given to the university by an alumnus of the school. In recognition for his help, the locker room at the University of Miami is named after Johnson.

Dwayne Johnson also founded the Dwayne Johnson Rock

Foundation in 2006, with the aim of improving the lives of at-risk children. The foundation provides a platform of hope and possibility for children hospitalized with medical disabilities, illnesses and disorders by providing them with access to healthcare and helping instill self-esteem in them. The foundation also has a physical fitness program which seeks to improve the health of children by teaching them about nutrition and healthy practices in order to help them achieve their fitness goals. The goal of the foundation, which works with children between infancy and the age of twenty-two, is to make every child smile.

Dwayne Johnson is also part of the board of directors of The Beacon Experience, whose aim is to encourage children to go beyond a high school education by offering programs that involve increased parental involvement, mentoring and special courses. Whenever he is on set, Dwayne Johnson also takes some time out to visit children's homes within the city where he is filming at the time. In addition to The Dwayne Johnson Rock Foundation and The Beacon Experience, Johnson also supports several other charities, including the Boot Campaign, Make-A-Wish Foundation, Until There's a Cure, Red Cross, Make The Difference Network, Kids Wish Network, Rush Philanthropic Arts Foundation, I Have a Dream Foundation, Parkinson Society Maritime Region,

Starlight Children's Foundation and many more. This is just part of his support for the many causes close to his heart, including At-Risk/Disadvantaged Youths, Children, Human Rights, Health, HIV and AIDS, Disaster Relief, Creative Arts, Cancer, Grief Support, Education, Veteran/Service Member Support, Parkinson's disease, and many more.

In 2017, rumors started doing rounds that Dwayne Johnson has plans to run for the presidency of the United States. The rumors were started by a Washington Post article which stated that if he were to run for president, there is a high chance that he would actually win. The public supported the idea until it got to Dwayne Johnson. He has stated in a few interviews that he is seriously considering running for president. However, with his tight movie schedule and the short time remaining to the next elections, do not expect to see Dwayne Johnson on the ballot in 2020. However, there is a serious possibility that he might one day run for the top office in the United States.

Since the age of 13, up to now, there has been one constant in Dwayne Johnson's life, one that has given him a sense of direction and discipline – the gym. Dwayne Johnson attributes everything that he has achieved today and the man that he is today to the gym. Hitting the gym kept him from joining gangs, helped him build the body that would help him in football, then wrestling and give him the appeal which would eventually make him a hero of the silver screen.

Every morning, Dwayne Johnson is always up by 3.30 am in preparation for a workout. If he's at his Florida home, by 4.00 am he is already outside the door for a 30 to 50 minute morning run. If he's in a hotel, the morning run will be replaced by 30 to 50 minutes of cardio on the elliptical cross trainer. From there, he takes breakfast before heading back to the gym for an hour of intense workouts. Only after these two hours of training does he start his day officially. He refers to the gym as his anchor, the thing that helps keep him grounded. Dwayne uses his Instagram posts to share his workouts with the world and inspire millions of people to get off the couch and live a healthier life.

With all the hard work he puts in, both in the gym and outside, it is no wonder that Dwayne Johnson has established himself as one of the greatest actors in the modern era. As he famously said, success always comes down to focus and effort, both of which are within our control.

Final Words

The life of Dwayne "The Rock" Johnson is the epitome of an inspiring story. In his life, there are several moments that threatened to turn his life into a tragedy; getting arrested, suffering an injury a few days away from being the first freshman to play for the college team, getting cut off from the Calgary Stampeders, getting rejected by WWE fans. However, none of these events were able to put Johnson down. From his teenage years, he created a vision of the kind of life he wanted to live and was ready to do whatever it took to achieve those dreams. As a teenager, he realized that all his idols worked hard on their bodies, and he made the decision to do the same. He has stuck with this decision to this day, more than three decades after making the decision. His determination and hard work has seen him transform himself from a child truant into one of the greatest actors of all time.

It is my hope that by reading this book, you have gotten a clear picture of the kind of mental toughness it takes to achieve your dreams, despite all the hurdles and obstacles that life places across your path. I also hope that through Dwayne Johnson's life, the book has provided you with a role model who is the embodiment of the kind of effort and determination you need to apply in your life if you want to become the best version of yourself. I encourage you to take the lessons you have learnt from this book and apply them in your life.

Thanks for checking out my book. I hope you found this of value and enjoyed it. If this was the case, head to my author page for more like this. Before you go, I have one small favor to ask…

Would you take 60 seconds and write a quick review about this book?

Reviews are the best way for independent authors (like me) to get noticed, sell more books, and it gives me the motivation to continue producing. I also read every review and use the feedback to write future revisions – and even future books. Thanks again.

Manufactured by Amazon.ca
Bolton, ON

17854906R00035